DAVID E. WHITE

How to Budget & Save

Unlock Financial Freedom: Simple Budgeting Strategies for Every Income Level

First edition

This book was professionally typeset on Reedsy.
Find out more at reedsy.com

Dedication

To Barbara, my loving wife, whose support and encouragement have been my guiding light, to Kelli, my cherished daughter and greatest motivation, and to my late Mother and Father who showed me what a budget looks like. "How to Budget & Save" is dedicated to you all, with all my love and deepest appreciation.

Contents

Introduction

In today's complex financial landscape, managing personal finances effectively has never been more critical. Whether you're striving to pay off debt, save for a significant purchase, or simply gain a better understanding of where your money goes each month, learning how to budget and save is the cornerstone of financial well-being. This book, "How to Budget & Save: Unlock Financial Freedom," is designed to provide practical, straightforward strategies to help individuals at any income level to take control of their finances.

The importance of budgeting and saving cannot be overstated. Budgeting helps you understand your financial situation, control your spending, and make informed financial decisions. Saving, on the other hand, provides security and peace of mind, allowing you to handle emergencies, invest in opportunities, and achieve your long-term financial goals.

Financial freedom—the state of having sufficient personal wealth to live without the need to work actively for basic necessities. This is a goal that everyone can aspire to. It offers the ability to make choices that lead to a fulfilling life, free from the stress and anxiety that financial instability can bring.

Chapter 1: Understanding Financial Principles

Learn the basics of income, expenses, assets, and liabilities, and the importance of financial literacy.

For effective money management, it is important that you understand these few basic financial concepts.

*Income:
This is the money you receive, which can come from various sources such as your salary, dividends, interest, and other earnings.

*Expenses:
These are the costs you incur in your daily life. They can be fixed (like rent or mortgage payments) or variable (like groceries and entertainment).

*Assets:
These are things you own that have value. They can include cash, investments, property, and other valuables.

*Liabilities:

These are your debts or financial obligations. They include things like loans, credit card balances, and mortgages.

*Financial Literacy:
The ability to understand and effectively use various financial skills, including personal financial management, budgeting, and investing.

Here are a few benefits of financial literacy:

A. Better Decision Making - When you understand financial principles, you're better equipped to make informed decisions about spending, saving, and investing. Financial literacy will significantly enhance your decision-making in various aspects of personal finance.

B. Informed Choices - Individuals with financial literacy are equipped to make well-informed decisions regarding their finances. They can evaluate the pros and cons of different financial products, such as loans, investments, and savings accounts, by understanding key concepts like interest rates, risk, and return. For example, knowing how compound interest works can help you choose the right investment that maximizes returns over time.

C. Effective Budgeting - Financial literacy aids in creating and maintaining effective budgets. It helps individuals track their income and expenses, allocate funds to essential and non-essential categories, and ensure that they live within their means. This prevents overspending and promotes disciplined saving habits.

D. Debt Management - A good understanding of financial principles enables individuals to manage their debt more effectively. They can distinguish between good and bad debt, prioritize paying off high-interest debt first, and avoid falling into debt traps. This knowledge reduces financial stress and prevents the long-term negative impacts of excessive debt.

E. Investment Decisions - Financially literate individuals can make sound investment decisions. They understand the importance of diversification, risk assessment, and long-term planning. This knowledge helps them build a robust investment portfolio that aligns with their financial goals and risk tolerance.

F. Financial Planning - Financial literacy is crucial for effective financial planning. It allows individuals to set realistic financial goals, plan for future needs such as retirement or education, and take proactive steps to achieve these goals. This includes saving, investing, and managing risks through insurance and other financial products.

G. Increased Savings - Knowledgeable individuals are more likely to save effectively and take advantage of investment opportunities.

Here are some of the ways that Financial Literacy will play a crucial role in enhancing your ability to save money effectively:

1. Understanding Compound Interest: Financial literacy helps individuals comprehend the power of compound interest. This knowledge encourages early and consistent savings, leading to substantial growth of savings over time. By understanding how

interest on savings can accumulate, people are more motivated to save regularly and start early.

2. Budgeting Skills: A key component of financial literacy is the ability to create and stick to a budget. By tracking income and expenses, individuals can identify areas where they can cut back on unnecessary spending and allocate more funds towards savings. Effective budgeting ensures that saving becomes a consistent habit rather than an occasional effort.

3. Setting Financial Goals: Financial literacy enables individuals to set specific, measurable, achievable, relevant, and time-bound (SMART) financial goals. When people have clear savings goals, such as an emergency fund, a down payment for a house, or retirement savings, they are more likely to save diligently to meet these targets. Goal setting provides a clear road map and motivation for consistent saving.

4. Risk Management: Financially literate individuals under-stand the importance of having an emergency fund to manage financial risks. They are more likely to prioritize saving for unexpected expenses, such as medical emergencies or job loss, which prevents them from falling into debt during tough times. This proactive approach to risk management ensures financial stability and security.

5.Investment Knowledge: Financial literacy includes under-standing different saving and investment options, such as high-yield savings accounts, certificates of deposit (CDs), and retirement accounts. With this knowledge, individuals can make informed decisions about where to place their savings to maximize returns while minimizing risks. Diversified investment strategies can significantly enhance the growth of savings over time.

H. Reduced Financial Stress - Understanding your finances can reduce anxiety and provide a greater sense of control over your financial future. Financial literacy significantly reduces financial stress by equipping individuals with the knowledge and skills needed to manage their money effectively.

Here are several ways it will help you Reduce Financial Stress:

1. Informed Decision Making: Financial literacy empowers individuals to make informed choices about spending, saving, and investing. When people understand their financial options, they can avoid unnecessary debt and financial pitfalls, leading to a more stable financial situation and reduced anxiety.

2. Budgeting and Planning: Knowledge of budgeting and financial planning allows individuals to track their income and expenses, set realistic financial goals, and create a plan to achieve them. This proactive approach to managing finances helps individuals feel more in control and less stressed about their financial future.

3. Emergency Preparedness: Financial literacy encourages the creation of an emergency fund, which acts as a financial safety net for unexpected expenses such as medical emergencies, car repairs, or job loss. Having this buffer reduces the stress associated with unforeseen financial challenges, providing peace of mind.

4. Long-Term Security: Financial literacy promotes the importance of saving for long-term goals, such as retirement. By understanding investment options and the benefits of starting early, individuals can build a secure financial future, reducing the worry about financial stability in later life.

I. Mindset Shift - Financial literacy will facilitate a crucial mindset shift, transforming how individuals perceive and manage their money. Achieving financial freedom starts with a mindset shift.

Developing a positive attitude towards money management involves several of these following key aspects:

1. Empowerment through Knowledge: Understanding financial concepts empowers individuals to take charge of their finances, leading to a sense of control and confidence. This proactive approach replaces feelings of helplessness with a strategic mindset.

2. Long-Term Thinking: Financially literate individuals develop a future-oriented perspective, focusing on long-term financial goals rather than immediate gratification. This shift promotes disciplined saving and investing habits essential for achieving financial stability and growth.

3. Responsibility and Accountability: Financial literacy encourages individuals to take responsibility for their financial decisions. By understanding the consequences of their actions, they become more accountable, making deliberate and informed choices about spending, saving, and investing.

4. Positive Behavioral Changes: With increased financial knowledge, individuals are more likely to adopt positive financial behaviors, such as budgeting, saving regularly, and avoiding unnecessary debt. These habits reduce financial stress and contribute to overall financial well-being.

J. Embracing Responsibility – When you accept that you are in control of your financial situation, this means you are taking responsibility for your spending and saving habits. One of the significant benefits of financial literacy is that it fosters a sense of responsibility regarding your personal finances. This involves several of the following key components.

1. Awareness of Financial Decisions: Financial literacy equips individuals with the knowledge to understand the impact of their financial decisions. This awareness helps them make choices that align with their long-term financial goals rather than impulsive decisions that could lead to financial distress.

2. Accountability: With financial literacy, individuals learn to take ownership of their financial actions. They understand the consequences of overspending, accumulating debt, or neglecting savings. This accountability encourages more disciplined financial behaviors, such as sticking to a budget and prioritizing essential expenses.

3. Proactive Management: Financially literate individuals are more likely to actively manage their finances by tracking their income, expenses, and savings. This proactive approach allows them to identify potential financial issues early and take corrective measures, thereby preventing minor problems from

escalating into significant financial crises .

4. Financial Independence: Embracing financial responsibility leads to greater financial independence. Individuals who understand and manage their finances effectively are less likely to rely on others for financial support, thus enhancing their ability to make autonomous life decisions.

K.Continuous Learning - Financial literacy fosters continuous learning by equipping individuals with the tools to adapt to ever-changing financial environments. This learning extends beyond basic financial concepts. It will encourage a proactive approach to personal finance management. By staying informed about new financial products, tax laws, investment opportunities, and economic trends. Now individuals can make better financial decisions and build long-term wealth. This ongoing education helps people to navigate financial complexities and improve their overall financial health.

L. Setting Realistic Expectations - Understand that financial improvement takes time and requires consistent effort. Setting achievable goals and celebrating small victories along the way can keep you motivated.

Chapter 2: Assessing Your Financial Situation

Conduct a personal financial audit, track your income and expenses, and identify your financial goals.

A personal financial audit is an essential first step in assessing your financial situation and gaining control of your finances.

Here are some important steps to execute:

1.Gather Financial Statements: Collect all your financial documents, including bank statements, credit card bills, loan documents, and investment records.

2.Calculate Net Worth: Determine your net worth by subtracting your total liabilities from your total assets.

3.Analyze Cash Flow: Review your income and expenses to understand where your money is going and identify areas for improvement.

4.Tracking Income and Expenses: Accurate tracking of income and expenses is crucial for effective budgeting. Here are some things to do &/or review.

*Manual Tracking: Use a notebook or spreadsheet to record every transaction.

*Digital Tools: Utilize apps and software like Mint, YNAB (You Need a Budget), or personal finance tools offered by your bank. These tools can automate the tracking process and provide useful insights into your spending habits.

*Identifying Financial Goals: Setting clear financial goals is key to achieving financial freedom. Financial goals can be categorized as Short-Term Goals which are objectives that can be achieved within a year, such as building an emergency fund, paying off a small debt, or saving for a vacation or Long-Term Goals which are objectives that take more than a year to achieve, such as saving for retirement, buying a house, or funding your children's education.

Here are some top resources for each of your financial assessment needs:

1.Financial Statements: The SEC's Beginners' Guide to Financial Statements is a comprehensive resource for understanding how to read and analyze financial statements, including income statements, balance sheets, and cash flow statements.

2.Calculating Net Worth: Investopedia's Guide on How to Calculate Your Net Worth is an excellent resource that provides detailed instructions on assessing your assets and liabilities to determine your net worth.

3.Analyzing Cash Flow: Harvard Business School Online's Guide on How Managers Use Financial Statements provides insights into analyzing cash flow statements, including the inflows and outflows of cash within a business context.

4.Tracking Income and Expenses: NerdWallet's Expense Tracker Guide offers practical advice and tools for effectively tracking your income and expenses, ensuring you maintain a balanced budget.

5.Manual Tracking: Dave Ramsey's Budgeting Tools and Tips are valuable for those who prefer to manually track their finances. Ramsey's methods emphasize discipline and detailed record-keeping to stay on top of your financial situation.

6.Digital Tools: Mint's Personal Finance App is highly recommended for digital tracking of your finances. It offers comprehensive features for monitoring spending, setting budgets, and tracking investments.

These resources provide a robust foundation for assessing various aspects of your financial situation and improving your financial literacy.

Chapter 3: Creating a Budget

Explore different types of budgets, and how to create and maintain one that works for you.

There are several types of budgets, each with its own approach and benefits.

1.Zero-Based Budgeting: This method involves allocating every dollar of your income to specific expenses, savings, or debt repayments. The goal is to have no money left unallocated at the end of the month.

2.Envelope System: This involves putting cash into envelopes designated for specific spending categories. Once the money in an envelope is gone, you cannot spend any more in that category.

3.50/30/20 Rule: This rule divides your income into three categories: 50% for needs, 30% for wants, and 20% for savings and debt repayment.

4.Steps For Creating A Budget: Creating a budget involves several steps such as.

*List Your Income Sources: Document all sources of income, including your salary, side jobs, and investment earnings.

*Categorize Your Expenses: Divide your expenses into fixed (e.g., rent, utilities) and variable (e.g., groceries, entertainment).

*Set Budget Limits: Assign realistic amounts to each category based on your past spending and future goals.

*Track Your Spending: Monitor your spending throughout the month to ensure you stay within your budget limits.

*Adjust as Necessary: If you find that you're consistently over-spending in certain categories, adjust your budget accordingly.

*Adjusting and Maintaining Your Budget: A budget is not a set-it-and-forget-it tool. Regular reviews and adjustments are necessary for long-term success.

*Monthly Reviews: At the end of each month, review your budget to see how well you stuck to it. Identify any areas where you overspent and consider adjusting your budget for the next month.

*Adjust for Life Changes: Your financial situation can change due to events like getting a new job, moving, or having a child. Be prepared to adjust your budget to accommodate these changes.

*Stay Flexible: Allow for some flexibility in your budget to accommodate unexpected expenses. Having a buffer can prevent these expenses from derailing your financial plan.

Here are some top resources for each budgeting method:

1. Zero-Based Budgeting: Dave Ramsey's Guide to Zero-Based Budgeting. Dave Ramsey's approach to zero-based budgeting is well-regarded. His guide provides a comprehensive explanation of how to allocate every dollar of your income to specific expenses, savings, and debt repayment categories.

2.Envelope System: Dave Ramsey's Envelope System. Dave Ramsey also champions the envelope system, which involves using physical envelopes to manage cash for different spending categories. His website provides detailed instructions and tips on implementing this system effectively.

3.50/30/20 Rule: Elizabeth Warren's 50/30/20 Budget Rule. The 50/30/20 rule was popularized by Senator Elizabeth Warren in her book "All Your Worth: The Ultimate Lifetime Money Plan." It provides a straightforward approach to budgeting by dividing income into needs (50%), wants (30%), and savings/debt repayment (20%).

4.Steps to Create a Budget: NerdWallet's Guide to Creating a Budget. NerdWallet offers a detailed step-by-step guide on how to create a budget. It includes tips on tracking expenses, setting financial goals, and adjusting your budget as needed to stay on track.

These resources provide comprehensive and practical advice on various budgeting methods, helping you choose the best approach for managing your finances effectively.

Chapter 4: Reducing and Managing Debt

Understand debt, its types, and strategies to reduce and manage it effectively.

Debt can be a significant obstacle to financial freedom, but understanding its nature and types can help you manage it effectively.

Here are a few important things that you should be aware of for reducing and managing debt:

*Secured Debt: This type of debt is backed by collateral, such as a mortgage or car loan. If you default on the loan, the lender can take the collateral.

*Unsecured Debt: This type of debt is not backed by collateral and includes credit card debt and personal loans. Because there's no collateral, interest rates on unsecured debt are typically higher.

*Interest Rates: The cost of borrowing money, expressed as a percentage of the loan amount. Higher interest rates increase the total amount you repay over time.

*Snowball Strategy For Reducing Debt: Focus on paying off your smallest debts first. This can build momentum and provide a psychological boost as you see debts disappearing.

*Avalanche Strategy For Reducing Debt: Focus on paying off debts with the highest interest rates first. This method saves money in the long run by reducing the amount of interest you pay.

*Debt Consolidation: Combine multiple debts into a single loan with a lower interest rate. This can simplify payments and reduce the total amount of interest paid.

*Managing Debt Effectively: To manage debt effectively and avoid future problems, consider the following tips.

*Avoid New Debt: Limit the use of credit cards and loans unless absolutely necessary. Pay cash whenever possible.

*Negotiate with Creditors: If you're struggling to make payments, contact your creditors to negotiate better terms. They may be willing to reduce your interest rate or offer a more manageable payment plan.

*Debt Management Plans (DMPs): These are offered by credit counseling agencies and involve consolidating your payments into a single monthly payment to the agency, which then distributes the funds to your creditors.

*Bankruptcy: As a last resort, consider bankruptcy. It can provide relief from overwhelming debt, but it also has significant long-term consequences on your credit and financial standing.

Here are some top resources for each aspect of reducing and managing debt:

1.Secured Debt: Investopedia's Guide to Secured Debt. This guide provides a comprehensive overview of what secured debt is, how it works, and examples such as mortgages and auto loans. It also discusses the implications and risks associated with secured debt.

2.Unsecured Debt: NerdWallet's Explanation of Unsecured Debt. NerdWallet offers a clear and detailed explanation of unsecured debt, including types like credit card debt, personal loans, and medical bills, and provides strategies for managing it.

3.Interest Rates: Consumer Financial Protection Bureau (CFPB) on Understanding Interest Rates. The CFPB provides in-depth resources to understand different types of interest rates, how they are calculated, and their impact on various loans and debts.

4.Strategies to Reduce Debt: National Foundation for Credit Counseling (NFCC) Tips on Reducing Debt. The NFCC offers a variety of strategies and tips for reducing debt, including budgeting, negotiating with creditors, and seeking professional advice.

5.Snowball Method: Dave Ramsey's Snowball Method Guide. Dave Ramsey is a well-known proponent of the debt snowball method. His guide explains how to prioritize paying off smaller debts first to build momentum and motivation.

6.Avalanche Method: NerdWallet's Avalanche Method Guide. NerdWallet provides a detailed explanation of the avalanche method, which focuses on paying off debts with the highest interest rates first to save money over time.

7.Debt Consolidation: Bankrate's Guide to Debt Consolidation. Bankrate offers an extensive guide on debt consolidation, discussing various options like personal loans, balance transfer credit cards, and home equity loans.

8.Managing Debt Effectively: Federal Trade Commission (FTC) on Managing Debt. The FTC provides comprehensive resources on managing debt effectively, including practical tips and warnings about scams.

9.Avoid New Debt: Investopedia's Tips on Avoiding New Debt. This article provides strategies to avoid falling into new debt, including tips on budgeting, living within your means, and using credit wisely.

10.Negotiate with Creditors: NerdWallet's Guide to Negotiating with Creditors. NerdWallet offers a practical guide on how to negotiate with creditors, including tips on preparing for negotiations and what terms you can seek to adjust.

11.Debt Management Plans: NFCC on Debt Management Plans. The National Foundation for Credit Counseling provides information on what debt management plans are, how they work, and how to enroll in one through their certified counselors .

12.Bankruptcy: United States Courts on Bankruptcy. The official website of the U.S. Courts provide detailed information on the bankruptcy process, different types of bankruptcy, and what to expect when filing.

These resources offer detailed and reliable information to help you understand and manage various aspects of debt effectively.

Chapter 5: Smart Money Management

Discover savings strategies, tips for cutting expenses, and ways to increase income.

Effective money management involves building savings to secure your financial future.

Here are some key strategies to execute for Smart Money Management:

*Emergency Fund: Aim to save at least three to six months' worth of living expenses. This fund provides a financial cushion in case of unexpected events like job loss or medical emergencies.

*High-Yield Savings Accounts: Keep your savings in a high-yield savings account to earn more interest compared to a regular savings account.

*Automate Savings: Set up automatic transfers from your checking account to your savings account. This ensures you consistently save money without thinking about it.

*Reducing unnecessary expenses can free up more money for savings and investments.

*Evaluate Your Spending: Review your expenses and identify non-essential spending. Consider cutting back on dining out, subscription services, and impulse purchases.

*Frugal Living: Adopt a frugal lifestyle by making mindful spending choices, such as buying second-hand items, using coupons, and taking advantage of sales and discounts.

*Energy and Utility Savings: Reduce your utility bills by implementing energy-saving practices, such as using energy-efficient appliances and unplugging devices when not in use.

*Side Hustles: Explore part-time jobs or freelance opportunities in areas like writing, graphic design, tutoring, or ridesharing. These can provide additional income without requiring a full-time commitment.

*Passive Income: Invest in opportunities that generate passive income, such as rental properties, dividend-paying stocks, or peer-to-peer lending. Passive income allows you to earn money with minimal effort.

*Career Advancement: Invest in your professional development by acquiring new skills or certifications that can lead to higher-paying job opportunities or promotions.

Here are some top resources for each listed aspect of Smart Money Management:

1.Emergency Fund: NerdWallet's Guide to Building an Emergency Fund. This comprehensive guide covers why an emergency fund is essential, how much to save, and strategies for building one quickly.

2.High Yield Savings Account: NerdWallet's Comparison of High Yield Savings Accounts. NerdWallet provides an up-to-date comparison of the best high yield savings accounts, including interest rates and account features.

3.Automate Savings: The Balance on How to Automate Your Savings. The Balance offers practical advice on setting up automatic transfers and using technology to ensure consistent saving habits.

4.Reducing Unnecessary Expenses: Investopedia's Tips on Cutting Unnecessary Expenses. Investopedia provides detailed strategies for identifying and cutting unnecessary expenses to improve financial health.

5.Evaluate Your Spending: Consumer Financial Protection Bureau (CFPB) on Tracking and Managing Expenses. The CFPB offers tools and tips for tracking and evaluating spending to gain better control over personal finances.

6.Frugal Living: The Simple Dollar's Guide to Frugal Living. The Simple Dollar provides extensive tips on adopting a frugal lifestyle, including practical advice on saving money in various areas of life.

7.Energy and Utility Savings: Energy.gov's Tips for Energy Efficiency. The U.S. Department of Energy offers a comprehensive guide to saving energy at home, which can significantly reduce utility bills.

8.Side Hustles: Side Hustle Nation's Guide to Starting a Side Hustle. This website provides a wealth of ideas and practical advice for starting and growing a side hustle to earn extra income.

9.Passive Income: Investopedia's Overview of Passive Income Strategies. Investopedia covers various passive income streams, including investments, rental income, and online businesses.

10.Career Advancement: Harvard Business Review on Career Development. HBR offers articles and advice on career advancement, including networking, skill development, and career planning.

These resources provide valuable information and practical tips to help you manage your money smartly and achieve financial stability.

Chapter 6: Setting and Achieving Long-Term Financial Goals

Learn goal-setting techniques and how to plan for major life events.

Looking At:

*Setting clear, actionable goals is crucial for financial success. Use the SMART goals framework to create effective financial goals.

-S / Specific: Clearly define your goal. For example, Save $25,000 for a house down payment.

-M / Measurable: Establish criteria to track progress. For example, Save $600 per month.

-A / Achievable: Set realistic goals that are within your reach.

-R / Relevant: Ensure your goals align with your broader financial objectives.

-T / Time-bound: Set a deadline for achieving your goal. For example, Save $25,000 in four years.

*Planning for Major Life Events: Prepare financially for significant life events such as..

1.Education: Save for your children's education using accounts like 529 plans, which offer tax advantages.

2.Home Purchase: Plan for buying a home by saving for a down payment, understanding mortgage options, and budgeting for associated costs like property taxes and maintenance.

3.Retirement: Start saving for retirement as early as possible. Utilize retirement accounts like 401(k)s or IRAs, and aim to contribute consistently to benefit from compound interest.

Remember to:

*Maintain Motivation: Motivation is key to achieving long-term financial goals.

*Track Progress: Regularly review your progress towards your goals. This can help you stay on track and make necessary adjustments.

*Celebrate Milestones: Recognize and reward yourself for reaching significant milestones. This can help maintain motivation and provide a sense of accomplishment.

*Stay Informed: Keep learning about personal finance and seek inspiration from others who have successfully achieved financial freedom.

Here are some top resources for setting and achieving long-term financial goals in each specified area:

1.SMART Goals: Mind Tools on SMART Goals. Mind Tools provides a detailed guide on setting SMART goals (Specific, Measurable, Achievable, Relevant, Time-bound), including examples and tips for effective goal setting. [Mind Tools - SMART Goals](https://www.mindtools.com/pages/article/smart-goals.htm)

2.Planning for Major Life Events: Fidelity's Guide to Financial Planning for Life Events. Fidelity offers comprehensive advice on planning financially for major life events such as marriage, having children, and career changes. [Fidelity - Financial Planning for Life Events](https://www.fidelity.com/viewpoints/personal-finance/planning-for-life-events)

3.Education: College Board's Resource on Financial Planning for Education. The College Board provides information on saving for college, financial aid, and budgeting for educational expenses. [College Board - Financial Planning for Education](https://bigfuture.collegeboard.org/pay-for-college)

4.Home Purchase: NerdWallet's Home Buying Guide. NerdWallet offers an extensive guide on the home buying process, including saving for a down payment, mortgage options, and budgeting for homeownership. [NerdWallet - Home Buying Guide](https://www.nerdwallet.com/article/mortgages/first-time-home-buyer-guide)

5.Retirement: AARP's Retirement Planning Resources. AARP provides tools, calculators, and articles to help with retirement planning, including savings strategies and retirement account management. [AARP - Retirement Planning](https://www.aarp.org/retirement/)

6.Maintaining Motivation: Forbes on Maintaining Financial Motivation. Forbes offers strategies and tips for staying motivated with long-term financial goals, including the importance of tracking progress and celebrating milestones.

7.Tracking Progress: Investopedia's Guide on Tracking Financial Progress. Investopedia provides advice on using tools and methods to monitor financial goals, including apps and spreadsheets for tracking savings, investments, and debt reduction.

8.Celebrating Milestones: The Balance on Celebrating Financial Milestones. The Balance discusses the importance of recognizing and celebrating financial achievements to maintain motivation and build positive financial habits. [The Balance - Celebrating Financial Milestones](https://www.thebalance.com/how-to-celebrate-financial-goals-453944)

9.Staying Informed:
  ▪Kiplinger's Personal Finance Magazine. Kiplinger's provides up-to-date information on personal finance, including articles on investing, saving, and economic trends to help you stay informed about financial matters. [Kiplinger - Personal Finance](https://www.kiplinger.com/personal-finance)
  ▪Carlozo & Company,P.A. Certified Public Accountant- Blog.. Unlock Hidden Savings: A Guide to Maximizing Tax Deductions

for Small Business Owners – Carlozo (https://www.carlozo.com)

These resources offer valuable insights and practical advice to help you set, achieve, and maintain long-term financial goals effectively.

Chapter 7: Tools and Resources

In today's environment, you can utilize technology to manage your finances more effectively.

Here are some suggested tools and apps:

*Budgeting Apps: Apps like Mint, YNAB (You Need a Budget), and PocketGuard help track spending, create budgets, and manage finances.

*Investment Tools: Platforms like Robinhood, E*TRADE, and Betterment offer easy access to investment opportunities and portfolio management.

*Debt Management Apps: Apps like Debt Payoff Planner and Undebt it help you create and track a debt repayment plan.

*Educational Resources: Expand your financial knowledge through various educational resources.

*Books: "Rich Dad Poor Dad" by Robert Kiyosaki, "The Total Money Makeover" by Dave Ramsey, and "Your Money or Your Life" by Vicki Robin and Joe Dominguez.

*Websites: Websites like Investopedia, NerdWallet, and The Balance offer comprehensive financial advice and tools.

*Courses: Online courses on platforms like Coursera, Udemy, and Khan Academy can provide in-depth financial education on topics ranging from budgeting to investing.

*Professional Advice: Know when to seek professional financial advice.

*Financial Advisors: Certified financial planners (CFPs) can provide personalized advice on a wide range of financial topics, from retirement planning to investment strategies.

*Tax Professionals: CPAs and tax advisors can help you navigate complex tax issues and optimize your tax situation.

*Credit Counselors: Nonprofit credit counseling agencies can assist with debt management and provide guidance on improving your credit score.

Other resources to consider:

*Education Resources: Jump$tart Coalition for Personal Financial Literacy. Jump$tart provides resources, tools, and materials to improve financial literacy among students from pre-kindergarten through college. [Jump$tart Coalition](https://www.jumpstart.org/)

*Financial Advisors: National Association of Personal Financial Advisors (NAPFA). NAPFA is a leading organization of fee-only financial advisors. Their website offers a tool to find qualified financial advisors who adhere to strict ethical standards. [NAPFA](https://www.napfa.org/)

*Tax Professionals: National Association of Tax Professionals (NATP). NATP provides resources to help individuals find qualified tax professionals. They offer a directory of members who adhere to high standards of ethics and professionalism. [NATP](https://www.natptax.com/)

*Credit Counselors: National Foundation for Credit Counseling (NFCC). NFCC is a leading non-profit organization providing credit counseling services. Their website offers a tool to find certified credit counselors who can assist with budgeting, debt management, and financial education. [NFCC](https://www.nfcc.org/)

These resources offer comprehensive support and guidance in their respective areas, making them valuable tools for readers looking to enhance their budgeting and saving strategies.

Conclusion

Recapping of Key Points:

Throughout this book, we've explored the essential steps to achieving financial freedom such as ...

*Understanding basic financial principles and developing a positive money mindset.

*Conducting a personal financial audit and tracking income and expenses.

*Creating and maintaining a budget tailored to your financial situation.

*Reducing and managing debt effectively.

*Implementing smart money management strategies, including saving, cutting expenses, and increasing income.

*Setting and achieving long-term financial goals.

*Utilizing tools, resources, and professional advice to support your financial journey.

Final Encouragement:

Achieving financial freedom is a journey that requires dedication, discipline, and continuous learning. By implementing some of the strategies outlined in this book, you are taking the first steps towards a more secure and fulfilling financial future. Remember, small changes can lead to significant improvements over time. Stay committed to your goals, and don't be afraid to seek help and adjust your strategies as needed.

▪️ Next Steps

Here are some practical steps you can take immediately to start your financial journey.

1.Conduct a personal financial audit to understand your current financial situation.

2.Choose a budgeting method that suits your lifestyle and begin tracking your income and expenses.

3.Set specific, measurable, achievable, relevant, and time-bound financial goals.

4.Implement debt reduction strategies if you have outstanding debts.

5.Start building an emergency fund and explore ways to increase your income.

6.Utilize financial tools and apps to streamline your money management.

7.Continue learning about personal finance through books, websites, and courses.

Your financial future is in your hands. By taking action today, you can unlock the financial freedom you've always dreamed of.

Notes:

1.Lusardi, A., & Mitchell, O. S. (2014). The Economic Importance of Financial Literacy: Theory and Evidence. *Journal of Economic Literature*, 52(1), 5-44. Retrieved from [AEAweb](https://www.aeaweb.org/articles?id=10.1257/jel.5 2.1.5)

2.Huston, S. J. (2010). Measuring Financial Literacy. *Journal of Consumer Affairs*, 44(2), 296-316. Retrieved from [Wiley Online Library](https://onlinelibrary.wiley.com/doi/abs/10.1111

/j.1745-6606.2010.01170.x)

3.Remund, D. L. (2010). Financial Literacy Explicated: The Case for a Clearer Definition in an Increasingly Complex Economy. *Journal of Consumer Affairs*, 44(2), 276-295. Retrieved from [Wiley Online Library](https://onlinelibrary.wiley.com/doi/abs/10.1111/j.1745-6606.2010.01169.x)

4.Hira, T. K. (2012). Promoting sustainable financial behaviour: Implications for education and research. *International Journal of Consumer Studies*, 36(5), 502-507. Retrieved from [Wiley Online Library](https://onlinelibrary.wiley.com/doi/10.1111/j.1470-6431.2012.01118.x)

5.Atkinson, A., & Messy, F. (2012). Measuring Financial Literacy: Results of the OECD / International Network on Financial Education (INFE) Pilot Study. *OECD Working Papers on Finance, Insurance and Private Pensions*, No. 15. OECD Publishing. Retrieved from [OECD iLibrary](https://www.oecd-ilibrary.org/finance-and-investment/measuring-financial-literacy_5k9csfs90fr4-en)

6.Lusardi, A., & Mitchell, O. S. (2014). The Economic Importance of Financial Literacy: Theory and Evidence. *Journal of Economic Literature*, 52(1), 5-44. Retrieved from [AEAweb](https://www.aeaweb.org/articles?id=10.1257/jel.52.1.5)

7.Huston, S. J. (2010). Measuring Financial Literacy. *Journal of Consumer Affairs*,44(2), 296-316. Retrieved from [Wiley Online Library](https://onlinelibrary.wiley.com/doi/abs/10.1111

/j.1745-6606.2010.01170.x)

8.Remund, D. L. (2010). Financial Literacy Explicated: The Case for a Clearer Definition in an Increasingly Complex Economy. *Journal of Consumer Affairs*, 44(2), 276-295. Retrieved from [Wiley Online Library](https://onlinelibrary.wiley.com/doi/abs/10.1111/j.1745-6606.2010.01169.x)

9.Hira, T. K. (2012). Promoting sustainable financial behaviour: Implications for education and research. *International Journal of Consumer Studies*, 36(5), 502-507. Retrieved from [Wiley Online Library](https://onlinelibrary.wiley.com/doi/10.1111/j.1470-6431.2012.01118.x)

10.Atkinson, A., & Messy, F. (2012). Measuring Financial Literacy: Results of the OECD / International Network on Financial Education (INFE) Pilot Study. *OECD Working Papers on Finance, Insurance and Private Pensions*, No. 15. OECD Publishing. Retrieved from [OECD iLibrary](https://www.oecd-ilibrary.org/finance-and-investment/measuring-financial-literacy_5k9csfs90fr4-en)

11.How Financial Literacy Affects Saving Behavior". *Journal of Economic Behavior & Organization*. Retrieved from [ScienceDirect](https://www.sciencedirect.com/science/article/pii/S0167268120301566)

12. Lusardi, A. (2019). Financial Literacy and the Need for Financial Education: Evidence and Implications. *Swiss Journal of Economics and Statistics*, 155(1), 1-8. Retrieved from [SpringerLink](https://link.springer.com/article/10.1186/s4193

7-019-0027-5)

13. "Financial Literacy and Its Impact on Investment Decisions". *Journal of Financial Counseling and Planning*. Retrieved from [AFCPE](https://afcpe.org/news-and-publications/journal-of-financial-counseling-and-planning/)

14.Lusardi, A., & Mitchell, O. S. (2014). The Economic Importance of Financial Literacy: Theory and Evidence. *Journal of Economic Literature*, 52(1), 5-44. Retrieved from [AEAweb](https://www.aeaweb.org/articles?id=10.1257/jel.52.1.5)

15.Huston, S. J. (2010). Measuring Financial Literacy. *Journal of Consumer Affairs*, 44(2), 296-316. Retrieved from [Wiley Online Library](https://onlinelibrary.wiley.com/doi/abs/10.1111/j.1745-6606.2010.01170.x)

16.Remund, D. L. (2010). Financial Literacy Explicated: The Case for a Clearer Definition in an Increasingly Complex Economy. *Journal of Consumer Affairs*, 44(2), 276-295. Retrieved from [Wiley Online Library](https://onlinelibrary.wiley.com/doi/abs/10.1111/j.1745-6606.2010.01169.x)

17. Hira, T. K. (2012). Promoting sustainable financial behavior: Implications for education and research. *International Journal of Consumer Studies*, 36(5), 502-507. Retrieved from [Wiley Online Library](https://onlinelibrary.wiley.com/doi/10.1111/j.1470-6431.2012.01118.x)

18.Atkinson, A., & Messy, F. (2012). Measuring Financial Literacy: Results of the OECD / International Network on Financial Education (INFE) Pilot Study. *OECD Working Papers on Finance, Insurance and Private Pensions*, No. 15. OECD Publishing. Retrieved from [OECD iLibrary](https://www.oecd-ilibrary.org/finance-and-investment/measuring-financial-literacy_5k9csfs90fr4-en)

19.Lusardi, A. (2019). Financial Literacy and the Need for Financial Education: Evidence and Implications. *Swiss Journal of Economics and Statistics*, 155(1), 1-8. Retrieved from [SpringerLink](https://link.springer.com/article/10.1186/s41937-019-0027-5)

20.Lusardi, A., & Mitchell, O. S. (2014). The Economic Importance of Financial Literacy: Theory and Evidence. *Journal of Economic Literature*, 52(1), 5-44. Retrieved from [AEAweb](https://www.aeaweb.org/articles?id=10.1257/jel.52.1.5)

21.Remund, D. L. (2010). Financial Literacy Explicated: The Case for a Clearer Definition in an Increasingly Complex Economy. *Journal of Consumer Affairs*, 44(2), 276-295. Retrieved from [Wiley Online Library](https://onlinelibrary.wiley.com/doi/abs/10.1111/j.1745-6606.2010.01169.x)

22.Hira, T. K. (2012). Promoting sustainable financial behavior: Implications for education and research. *International Journal of Consumer Studies*, 36(5), 502-507. Retrieved from [Wiley Online Library](https://onlinelibrary.wiley.com/doi/10.1111/j.1470-6431.2012.01118.x)

23.Lusardi, A. (2019). Financial Literacy and the Need for Financial Education: Evidence and Implications. *Swiss Journal of Economics and Statistics*, 155(1), 1-8. Retrieved from [SpringerLink](https://link.springer.com/article/10.1186/s4193 7-019-0027-5)

24.Lusardi, A., & Mitchell, O. S. (2014). The Economic Importance of Financial Literacy: Theory and Evidence. *Journal of Economic Literature*, 52(1), 5-44. Retrieved from [AEAweb](https://www.aeaweb.org/articles?id=10.1257/jel.5 2.1.5)

25.Remund, D. L. (2010). Financial Literacy Explicated: The Case for a Clearer Definition in an Increasingly Complex Economy. *Journal of Consumer Affairs*, 44(2), 276-295. Retrieved from [Wiley Online Library](https://onlinelibrary.wiley.com/doi/abs /10.1111/j.1745-6606.2010.01169.x)

26.Hira, T. K. (2012). Promoting sustainable financial behavior: Implications for education and research. *International Journal of Consumer Studies*, 36(5), 502-507. Retrieved from [Wiley Online Library](https://onlinelibrary.wiley.com/doi/10.1111/j.14 70-6431.2012.01118.x)

27.Lusardi, A. (2019). Financial Literacy and the Need for Financial Education: Evidence and Implications. *Swiss Journal of Economics and Statistics*, 155(1), 1-8. Retrieved from [SpringerLink](https://link.springer.com/article/10.1186/s4193 7-019-0027-5)

28.Atkinson, A., & Messy, F.-A. (2012). Measuring Financial

Literacy

29.Results of the OECD / International Network on Financial Education (INFE) Pilot Study

30.OECD Working Papers on Finance, Insurance and Private Pensions

31.No. 15. Retrieved from [OECD iLibrary](https://www.oecd-ili brary.org/finance-and-investment/measuring-financial-liter acy_5k9csfs90fr4-en)

32.Carlozo & Company,P.A. Certified Public Accountant- Blog.. Unlock Hidden Savings: A Guide to Maximizing Tax Deductions for Small Business Owners - Carlozo (https://www.carlozo.com)

About the Author

About the Author: With over 21 years of experience as a multiple restaurant owner, David E. White brings a wealth of practical financial knowledge to the table. Before retiring, David navigated a diverse career path, including high school, college, graduate school, and a distinguished tenure in the U.S. Army. This journey continued through various corporate management positions, each contributing to a deep understanding of budgeting and saving.

Now enjoying the leisurely pace of retirement, where every day feels like a Saturday or Sunday, David shares the hard-earned wisdom of financial management. This book is a testament to his expertise and a practical guide for anyone looking to achieve financial freedom.

During the journey to retirement, David mastered essential financial skills, including:

*Conducting personal financial audits to gain clarity on current financial standings.

*Selecting a budgeting method tailored to individual lifestyle and rigorously tracking income and expenses.

*Setting specific, measurable, achievable, relevant, and time-bound (SMART) financial goals.

*Implementing effective debt reduction strategies.

*Building a emergency fund and discovering avenues to boost income.

*Utilizing financial tools and apps to simplify money management.

*Continuously learning about personal finance through books, websites, and courses.

In "How to Budget and Save" David distills these strategies into simple, actionable steps, empowering readers to take control of their finances, no matter their income level.